Ozzy
and the
Baby Birds

Diann L. Tongco

DEDICATION

For Christopher Doyle
and his brave son, Thomas, my grandson.
I love you both.

Ozzy the curly-coated retriever was a good dog. He liked long walks in the forest and playing with his toys. But sometimes he was bored.

One day a pair of birds started to build a nest on his deck. Ozzy loved to watch them work. The birds were not afraid of the big dog.

The birds were chickadees. They made their nest and laid four speckled eggs. Ozzy was happy. He was even happier when all the eggs hatched.

Every day Ozzy watched the chickadee parents feed their babies and keep them warm and safe.

One day a big black crow
saw the baby birds. He
thought they looked tasty.

The crow and his friends
came to scare the bird
parents and eat the little
chicks.

Ozzy barked at them. The chickadee parents cheeped and flapped their wings at the crows.

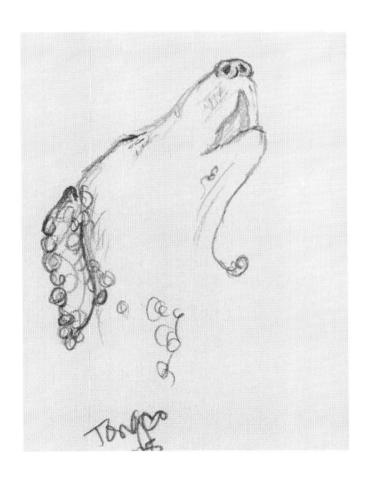

The crows were angry and made a lot of noise but Ozzy was brave and protected the baby birds.

The chickadee parents
were happy that their
babies were safe.

Ozzy was happy to have his bird friends around for a little longer. He watched them every day.

In a few days the baby birds learned to fly and Ozzy said goodbye to his little friends.

The chickadees came back
to visit sometimes and
Ozzy still kept watch to
keep the hungry crows
away.

THE END

ACKNOWLEDGMENTS

Thank you to my daughter Rita Tongco for encouraging me to join in her art project exchange on Facebook. This book might never have existed if not for her enthusiasm. Thanks also to Ozzy, my curly-coated retriever, for serving as my sometime muse and frequent companion. Finally, thank you to the black-capped chickadees who nested on the patio in my new fuchsia and captured my imagination.

This story is based on true events.

ABOUT THE AUTHOR

Diann L. Tongco is an animal lover, dog owner and proud mom and grandmother. She's always loved to draw and tell stories. Here she combines those passions to entertain her youngest grandchild.
Diann lives with her partner, Nick, and their curly-coated retriever, Ozzy, on Puget Sound in Washington where she revels in the gray skies, tall trees and rainy days...
and black-capped chickadees.

31636465R00016

Printed in Great Britain
by Amazon